# sculpturing with wax

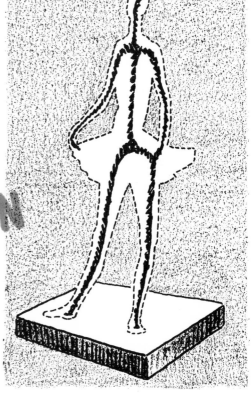

by <u>Maria and Louis</u>
<u>Di Valentin</u>

**STERLING**
**PUBLISHING CO., INC.**   **NEW YORK**

*Oak Tree Press Co., Ltd.*
Distributed by WARD LOCK, Ltd.,  London & Sydney

SAUNDERS OF TORONTO, Ltd., Don Mills, Canada

**LITTLE CRAFT BOOK SERIES**

## Little Craft Book Series

Balsa Wood Modelling
Bargello Stitchery
Beads Plus Macramé
Big-Knot Macramé
Candle-Making
Cellophane Creations
Ceramics by Slab
Coloring Papers
Corrugated Carton Crafting
Crafting with Nature's Materials
Creating Silver Jewelry with Beads
Creating with Beads
Creating with Burlap
Creating with Flexible Foam
Creative Lace-Making with Thread and Yarn
Cross Stitchery
Curling, Coiling and Quilling

Enamel without Heat
Felt Crafting
Finger Weaving: Indian Braiding
Flower Pressing
Folding Table Napkins
Hooked and Knotted Rugs
How to Add Designer Touches to Your Wardrobe
Ideas for Collage
Junk Sculpture
Lacquer and Crackle
Leathercrafting
Macramé
Make Your Own Elegant Jewelry
Making Paper Flowers
Making Shell Flowers
Masks
Metal and Wire Sculpture
Model Boat Building

Monster Masks
Nail Sculpture
Needlepoint Simplified
Off-Loom Weaving
Organic Jewelry You Can Make
Potato Printing
Puppet-Making
Repoussage
Scissorscraft
Scrimshaw
Sculpturing with Wax
Sewing without a Pattern
Starting with Stained Glass
String Things You Can Create
Tole Painting
Trapunto: Decorative Quilting
Whittling and Wood Carving

Photographs by Fred Cerfeda

# Contents

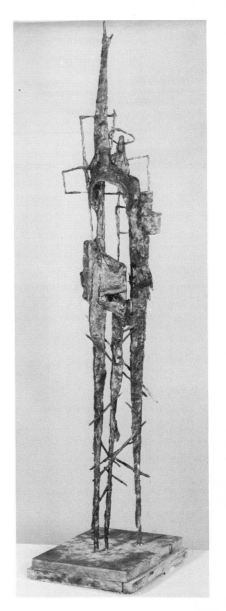

# Before You Begin

Since ancient times, wax has had many valuable and diverse uses. Wax was used by the Egyptians, Greeks, and Romans to make masks for death portraits and for sacred images, as well as for effigies of enemies. During the Middle Ages in Europe sorcerers melted wax figures of people toward whom their incantations were aimed, in front of a slow-burning fire. Wax was also used as a cosmetic in ancient Egypt and is still used today in face creams. The Egyptians also employed it as a vehicle to hold color for their encaustic paintings.

In the 19th century, wax dolls came into fashion, and so did life-size figures of famous and infamous people, such as the world-renowned waxworks of Madame Tussaud in London.

Today, wax serves an extraordinary number of purposes: to name a few, it is used as a *resist* in the batik process, as an *adhesive* in stained-glass windows, as a *binder* in mosaics and collages, and as a *mould* for plastics. As a *protective agent* against moisture, it is applied

Illus. 1. An abstract figure in wax.

to a variety of surfaces from milk containers to paintings. All in all, wax is one of the most versatile of substances. All sculptors have at one time or another worked with wax, from Michelangelo to Jacques Lipschitz.

The most important quality of wax is its plasticity. It is an ideal sculptural material because it can be poured, carved, or modelled with the fingers, and it won't warp, peel, flake or chip.

Actually, the term "wax" applies to a number of animal and vegetable substances, and some mineral hydrocarbons. All waxes have a characteristic dull lustre and greasy texture, and at ordinary temperatures are solid and somewhat brittle, but can be cut easily with a knife. Wax is insoluble in water and becomes soluble only when its molecular structure is altered by the addition of a foreign material such as alcohol, ether, or turpentine, or by *excessive* heat, in which case it melts and decomposes. Moderate heating, however, softens wax to a malleable consistency, and it is because of this quality that wax sculpturing can be performed.

The most common wax is beeswax, which is secreted by bees in constructing their hives. Although beeswax is secreted white, it soon turns yellow with age. Most of the beeswax you can purchase has undergone a bleaching to restore its pearly appearance. For modelling purposes, dilute beeswax with Venetian turpentine in a proportion that will make it just malleable enough.

There are also synthetic waxes which are called microcrystallines, and come closer to the color and consistency of beeswax than any other wax. These come in slabs and are generally the least expensive waxes. Pure beeswax is several times as expensive per pound as synthetics. Undiluted microcrystalline waxes are especially suitable for carving.

Paraffin is a white, translucent, waxy substance which is distilled from petroleum and has a low melting point—anywhere from 86° F. (30° C.) for soft paraffin, and from 125° F. (52° C.) and up for hard paraffin. Straight paraffin is excellent for carving.

Pink dental wax, which is used in bridges and plates, is also suitable for your wax sculpturing, as are several of the synthetic waxes produced by various petrochemical companies. You can use most of these for either carving or modelling.

Modelling wax, which is more expensive than the synthetics, is a mixture of bleached beeswax and an equal amount of paraffin. Dyes are often added during the processing of it. Modelling wax is not only used for modelling, but also for casting.

As a medium for sculpture, there are many different ways wax can be worked. For small sculptures, you can pinch, smooth, and mould a lump with your hands and fingers. Or, you can build a piece up with coils as in claywork. Solid blocks of wax can be carved just as if they were wood or marble.

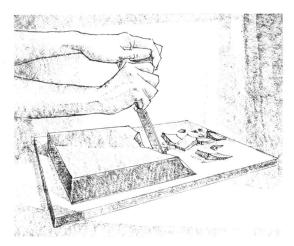

Illus. 2. Break off pieces of wax with a cutting tool.

# Melting Wax

You will start with wax in slabs, blocks, or sheets. You can also use candles. Save old and half-used candles; add to beeswax in the proportion of anywhere from one-third to one-half. To melt wax, break off small pieces from the block or slab with a cutting tool (Illus. 2). Place them into the upper part of a double boiler, such as the canned heat (Sterno) type in Illus. 3 or in a regular double boiler on an electric hot plate (Illus. 4). Never place wax in a vessel that is directly over the source of heat.

Pour enough water into the lower part of the boiler to just barely touch the bottom of

Illus. 3. Melt the wax in either a Sterno double boiler or . . .

Illus. 4. . . . in a regular double boiler on a hot plate.

Illus. 5. Always use a low heat to melt wax, and be sure never to let it boil.

the upper pot containing the wax. Use a low heat to melt the wax, and as soon as it is completely molten, remove the double boiler from the stove. *Never over-heat or boil the wax* —you will alter its chemical properties and render it unusable for your purposes.

You will have plenty of time while the wax is melting, to take a large sheet of aluminum foil and either spray it with silicone (Illus. 6), or brush it with a light layer of vegetable oil. Make sure that you cover the entire sheet. Then bend up all four sides slightly as shown in Illus. 6.

As soon as you remove the wax from the

Illus. 6. Spray a sheet of aluminum foil with silicone, or brush on a layer of oil to hold the melted wax.

Illus. 7. After adding turpentine, let cool for a few minutes and then pour onto the aluminum sheet so that it forms an even layer.

Illus. 8. After the wax congeals, carefully peel it off the sheet in one piece.

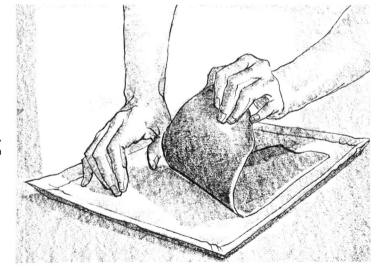

Illus. 9. Then lay the wax on a board or work-table.

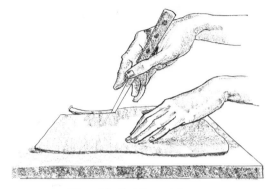

Illus. 10. Cutting strips.

heat, mix in turpentine with a wooden stick. Remember, the more turpentine you add, the softer the wax will be.

Allow the wax to cool for several minutes and then pour it out onto the aluminum sheet, taking care not to pour onto one spot only. Rather, pour all round the sheet so you will have an even layer of wax (Illus. 7).

When the wax congeals, peel it carefully from the aluminum sheet (Illus. 8). You should have no trouble with sticking if the sheet was properly oiled. Then place the wax on your work-table or board. You can now cut the wax into strips (Illus. 10), or roll it into sausage shapes (Illus. 11), or form it into lumps, squares or whatever shapes you wish (Illus. 12).

Illus. 12. After melting, you can work the wax into any forms and shapes you wish.

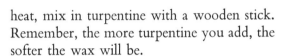

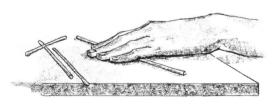

Illus. 11. Rolling "sausages."

Illus. 13. An apple is a modified sphere.

Since all sculpture is based on variations and modifications of simple geometric forms—the sphere, cube, cone, cylinder, etc., you can quickly and easily make a simple sculpture using everyday subjects, such as fruit and vegetables.

## Spheres

Think of as many kinds of fruit as you can that fall into a spherical category—apples, oranges, grapefruit, melons. Choose one as a model, say an apple. Set the apple up in a good light and study it carefully. It is always helpful when searching out a basic geometric form or forms to make a pencil or charcoal sketch of the object. This eliminates the distraction of details and points up the basic

elements. You will notice that although the apple is not a "true" sphere, it is a modified one.

Shape a large lump of wax into a ball with your hands. With your fingers, make the necessary modifications depending upon the shape of the apple model. For example, one apple will be squatter and have rounder "shoulders" than another. Add and subtract, bend or indent, where needed. You will find that the plasticity of wax lends itself to this and responds immediately to the softening and smoothing pressure of your hands and fingers.

Grapes are fun to make and you can sculpture an entire cluster in a short time (Illus. 14). Roll a small round piece of wax between the palms of your hands until you

10

have achieved the slightly oval shape of one type of grape. Make a whole bunch of them and then make the stems. First, form the main stem by rolling a strip of wax with both hands on a table. Then make small individual stems for each grape. Stick the stems onto the grapes and then attach each to the main stem by pressing.

To make a grape leaf, outline the general shape, using a pointed tool, on a flat sheet of wax (Illus. 15). Then carefully cut straight through, all round the outline. For your first attempts, keep the outline as simple as possible

Illus. 14. Using your hands only, make a cluster of grapes.

Illus. 15. Make the grape leaf as simple and undetailed as possible.

Illus. 16. The completed still life.

and avoid fussy details. Then indent the central vein with the tool and attach the leaf to the end of the main grape stem.

Illus. 17. Acorns have an elliptical shape.

Illus. 18. This vase is almost a perfect sphere.

Modelling a portrait is one of the most exciting projects for a beginner. (See page 34.)

Illus. 19.

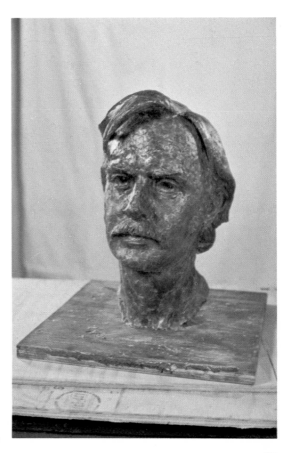

Illus. 20.

Illus. 21. A banana is a modified cylinder, as you can see in Illus. 22.

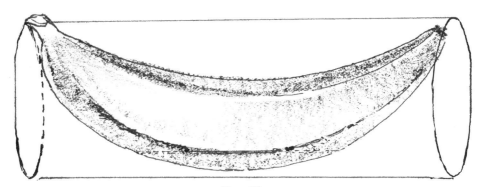

Illus. 22.

Illus. 23.

## Cylinders

Many objects fall into a more or less cylindrical form, and you must develop a discerning eye to be able to recognize them. This is true of all objects you intend to sculpture. Be sure to study the model carefully—it will make your finished object far more successful than if you just plunge in carelessly.

At first glance, you might not realize a banana is a modified cylinder because of its curvature. However, in your mind's eye, try to see the banana as it would appear straightened out. Do you see a cylinder now? Begin by rolling out a thick sausage of wax on your work-table. Press it and guide it just as though rolling dough.

When you have achieved the general size in length and thickness, curve the two ends. Then, to form the flattened sections of the skin, use a spatula and press on the wax to form rather sharp ridges (see Illus. 22) between each flat segment. Converge the ridges to a blunt end. The other end, where the stem is, can be modelled with the fingers.

Another modified cylinder is the carrot (Illus. 23). Again, roll out the wax as you did with the banana, but concentrate on modelling a tapering form. Achieve the carrot's characteristic bumps and general unevenness with your fingers.

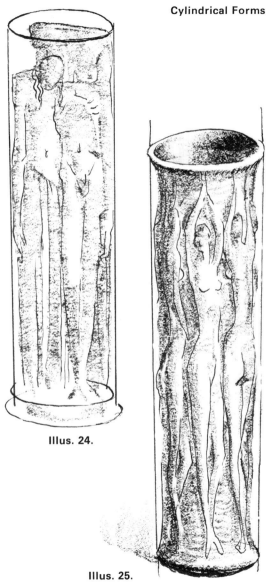

**Illus. 24.**

**Illus. 25.**

15

Illus. 26. An abstract figure in wax demonstrates the use of the internal armature as support for the sculpture.

Illus. 27. The armature for this sculpture utilizes both wire and copper tubing.
(See page 31.)

Illus. 28. Always break down objects into their basic forms before starting your sculpture.

## Cones

A great variety of objects fit into the cone shape, but for your first experiments, choose a pear to sculpture. Make a sketch of the model first. Even though the conical form of the pear is obvious to you, if you get in the habit of always breaking down an object into its basic form, you will be a better sculptor. It is important to remember that sculpture begins with the *inner structure*.

Shape a large lump of wax in a slightly elongated ball. Now observe the pear model carefully. Note whether it leans to one side, whether one side is fuller than the other. Note any surface irregularities—bumps,

indentations. Start moulding with your fingers. Add wax where needed and subtract where it is too full. Press the wax on with your thumb where you want to add and indent with a heavy pressure of both thumbs where you want to subtract. Keep comparing your progress with the model, and when you feel satisfied with its form, add a small cylinder of wax for a stem.

Illus. 29. A pear is a modified cone.

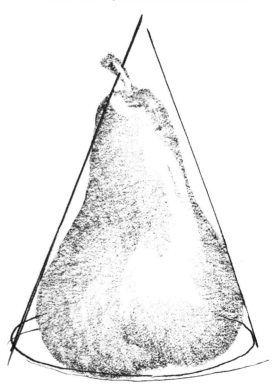

# Modified Cones

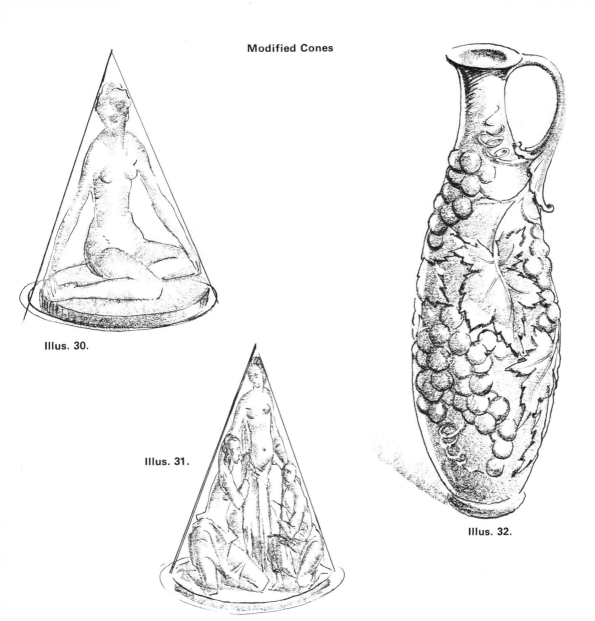

Illus. 30.

Illus. 31.

Illus. 32.

19

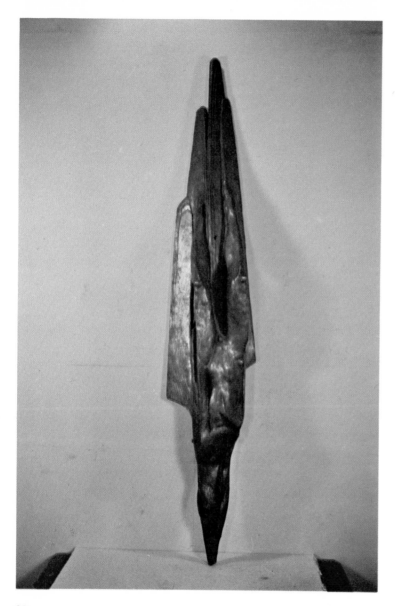

Illus. 33. Free-form sculpture as well as representational can always be broken down into a basic form. Note this modified cone shape.

Illus. 34. A sitting wax "poodle" takes the form of a modified cone.

**Illus. 35. A pepper is a modified cube.**

## Combining Forms

Experiment first with other geometric forms—the rectangle, the square, the cube—carefully selecting models that fall into each category, such as the pepper shown in Illus. 35.

When you have explored each basic form, look for models that combine shapes. For example, the mushroom (Illus. 37) is a half-sphere and a cylinder. An ice-cream cone is a half-sphere and a cone.

As you broaden the scope of your wax sculpturing to more complex models, such as the human figure and animals, you will gradually come to understand that almost anything you choose for sculpturing is composed of combinations of the basic geometric forms (Illus. 38).

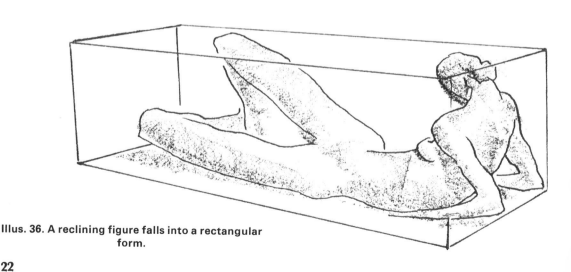

**Illus. 36. A reclining figure falls into a rectangular form.**

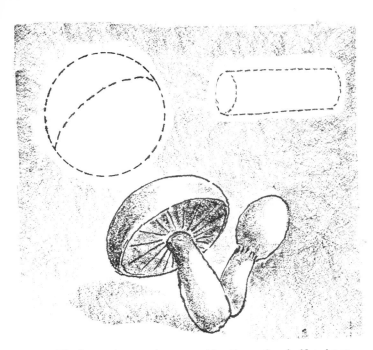

Illus. 37. A mushroom is a combination of a half-sphere and a cylinder.

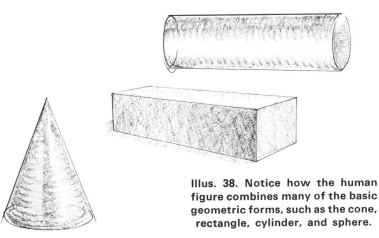

Illus. 38. Notice how the human figure combines many of the basic geometric forms, such as the cone, rectangle, cylinder, and sphere.

Illus. 39. Note how this figure is conceived as an extended cone.

Illus. 40. This reclining figure was modelled over a wire and copper tubing armature. (See the armature on page 31.)

Illus. 41. An example of how the armature is incorporated into the sculpture itself. Wire and tubing are excellent for sculpture that has extended parts.

# Tools

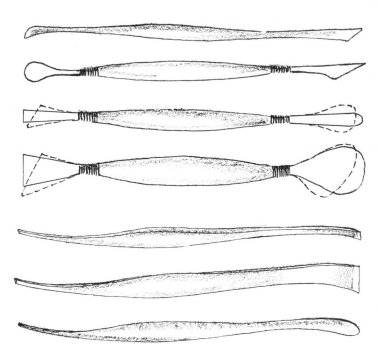

Illus. 42. You will need both wooden and wire tools for your wax modelling.

Now that you have discovered the joys of working with wax and have the satisfaction of having produced a quantity of simple sculptures using nothing more than your own hands, you will want to progress to a higher level. There are certain tools that you will need to acquire for your next step—modelling. However, while tools are useful, a large number of tools will not automatically make you a good sculptor. No tool in the world is a substitute for a pair of sensitive hands.

Illus. 42 shows a variety of modelling tools.

To cut away, subtract, remove, and to make hollows or concave areas, use a looped wire tool. Which one you use depends upon the size and type of the area to be removed. The larger wire tools are used to establish wide planes and areas, while the small wire tools are for digging out in small places.

Use wooden tools to add wax and for flattening it into place. Again, the larger tools are for adding large quantities and the small wooden tools for adding wax in small detailed places.

# Armatures

An armature is an understructure or skeleton which sculptors use whenever they plan to make anything except a very small sculpture. Ready-made armatures are available at art supply shops in different sizes for a variety of uses—from heads to animals. However, since you will probably want to give vent to your own imaginative forms and poses, you can make your own armatures very easily.

Use wood, wire, pipe, or plaster. Most sculptors planning life-size projects prefer to work over a plaster armature (Illus. 43). Plaster allows for a firm sturdy core over

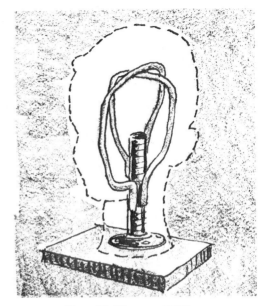

**Illus. 44. Pipe armature.**

**Illus. 43. Plaster armature.**

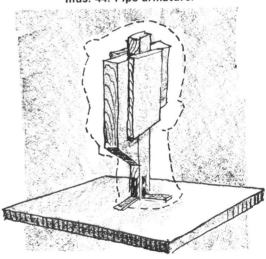

**Illus. 45. Wood armature.**

Illus. 46. Wax is an ideal medium for bas-relief sculpture. (See page 43.)

Illus. 47. For sculpture in which you want to suggest movement, such as for the dancers shown here, use wire and copper tubing for your armature.

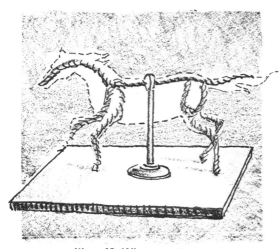

Illus. 48. Wire armature.

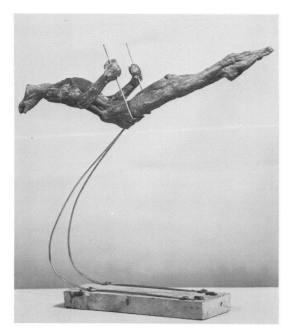

which to model the wax. Simply pile the plaster onto a block of wood to roughly resemble the shape of the object you intend to sculpture. The wood block will have to be attached to a heavy, flat baseboard (Illus. 43).

When planning not-too-large a sculpture, you might use a combination of wood and wire. Wire and flexible copper tubing are excellent when your piece has extended limbs or other parts, because they bend and give to suggest movement.

You can also effectively incorporate the armature into the sculpture itself. When the design itself demands external support such as "Man in the Swing" (Illus. 49), not only has the wax been layered over the wire armature for the extended arms and legs, but the wire swing serves as added support for the upper part of the sculpture.

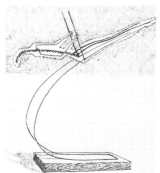

Illus. 49a.

Illus. 49. Here, the armature is incorporated into the design of the sculpture.

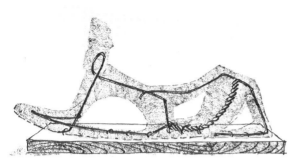

Illus. 50. Armature for color Illus. 40, made of wire and copper tubing.

An important thing to remember is always to make sure you are making your armature

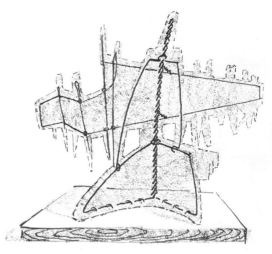

Illus. 51. Armature for color Illus. 27, also made of wire and tubing.

the right size—neither too large, nor too small. You must allow for a $\frac{1}{4}$-inch layer of wax.

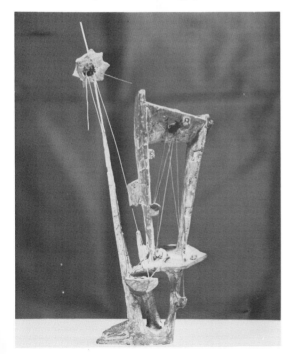

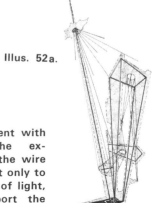

Illus. 52a.

Illus. 52. "Experiment with Light." Here, the externalized part of the wire armature serves not only to exemplify the rays of light, but also to support the upper part of the sculpture.

Illus. 53 and Illus. 54. Here are two examples of the use of a basic cylindrical form to express both a representational figure (left) and an abstract figure (right).

Illus. 55. In order to create a wax torso such as this one, a knowledge of anatomy is important. (See page 34.)

Illus. 56. See the completed portrait in color in Illus. 19.

# Modelling

One of the most exciting modelling projects for a beginner is making a head. If the head you plan is smaller than life-size, you will probably not need an armature or support inside. However, it is advisable to do a life-size head first because you can make an easier study of proportions. If you do a smaller-than-life head or a much larger head, you will need proportional dividers (Illus. 57) to translate the measurements from the model to the workpiece. However, you *will* in any case need calipers (Illus. 58) for accurate measuring.

In order to sculpture, or model, any living creature whether human or animal, you must acquire a certain knowledge and awareness of anatomy. If you wish, purchase some inexpensive anatomical plaster casts which are sold as study pieces—heads, feet, eyes, noses, hands, etc. These are also available in vinyl plastic. You should also study photographs, look carefully at your own head from all sides and angles in mirrors, or better still, have someone pose for you.

Prepare (page 6) as much wax as you will need for a life-size head. Work it with your hands into a large lump and set it on a work stand or table (Illus. 59). If you do not want to invest in a professional revolving table, hunt up an old piano stool which you can turn easily while working. A revolving stand

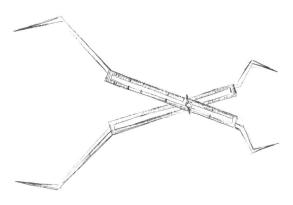

Illus. 57. Proportional dividers.

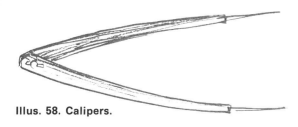

**Illus. 58. Calipers.**

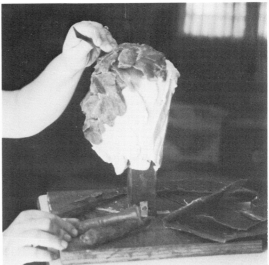

**Illus. 60. Massing wax on the armature.**

is particularly useful if you are doing a self-portrait where you must sit still and use mirrors in order to get front, side and back views.

If you are using an armature, mass the wax round it in the approximate size needed, using sausages or pellets of wax. For a simple head in a straight position, you need only a flat board with an upright in the middle. If you want, you can then use plaster or not. If you do, shellac the plaster before you add the wax, so it will stick better.

**Illus. 59. Modelling stands.**

### Measuring

Now, using calipers, take measurements of your model and establish certain critical points such as:
- from the top of the head to the chin;
- from the tip of the chin to the start of the throat;
- from the top of the head to the base of the neck in back;
- from ear to ear—over the top of the head and round the back;
- from the top of head to the brow;
- from the top of head to each ear.

Continue measuring all round and up and

Illus. 61. This grouping of figures falls into one of the basic forms—the rectangle.

down. As you measure each distance, mark it off in the wax with toothpicks. From the side view, note that the end of the skull in back is in line with the tip of the nose in front, that the top of the ear is in line with the eyebrow. Observe as many such relationships as you can.

Now that you have a start toward making your portrait, you must stop and consider the important structural elements of the head —the bones, muscles, and features.

## The Skull

Look at either a plaster cast of a skull or study the skull in Illus. 62. Make a sketch of a skull. Start with an oval or, if you prefer, with a circle, and modify it. Draw it from various angles—from above, from the front, from below—but just in outline form.

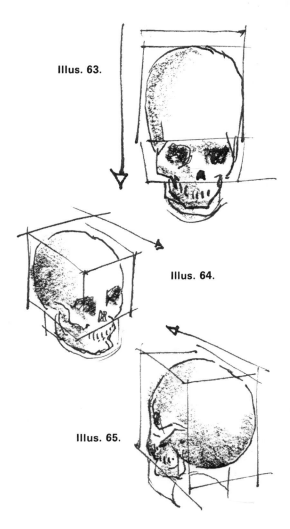

Illus. 63.

Illus. 64.

Illus. 65.

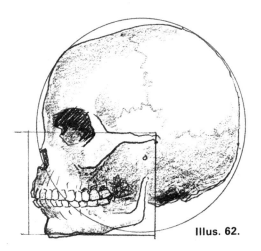

Illus. 62.

After you have made several sketches, draw the skull as a rectangular box with a smaller box under it (Illus. 63). Do this also from various angles. You can see from these

37

exercises that the skull is not really an oval, a circle, or a rectangle. However, it is a combination and modification of these geometric forms.

## The Muscles

Everyone, whether he knows it or not, has a real "skullcap." It consists of a tight-fitting inner skin that extends from the forehead to the back of the skull. On the forehead the cap ends in two frontal muscles which allow you to raise your eyebrows. Below these muscles on the top of the nose are two frowning muscles. The nose has a variety of muscles, particularly two long muscles on each side that go down to the mouth which pull up the upper lip. Two more pull the corners of the mouth up and out. The mouth is itself a muscle. The largest and strongest of the facial muscles are the chewing muscles which cover the lower part of the cheekbones and run along the jaws towards the chin.

Various muscles make up the chin and help in swallowing and the opening of the jaw.

Circular muscle fibres surround the eye. The ear has no muscles.

The shapes, forms and development of the muscles of the face vary with each person so that the face itself is almost impossible to describe.

Now let's look at the parts of the head you can actually see.

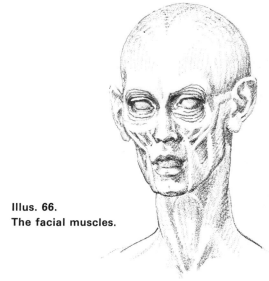

**Illus. 66.**
**The facial muscles.**

## The Nose

The nose is a vital part of the face. Although you probably think of it as protruding from the face, it is actually set into it as well. Look at yourself carefully in profile in a mirror.

The nose is made up of a series of wedges. Both sides of the nose slope down from the bridge. The bridge narrows below the bony part and sinks in where the bulbous cartilaginous part flares out. The end of the nose has many small planes and delicate curves. Notice that the nostrils are not round.

## The Mouth

The upper lip grows out from under the half-way mark between the tip of the nose and innermost part of the nostril. The corner of the mouth is usually on a line with the inset of the nose depending upon the arch of the teeth and how wide the mouth is.

The shape of the mouth is controlled by the shape of the upper and lower jaws. If the jaws are very curved, the lips will curve over them. The two lips are entirely different from each other. The upper has a central peak with soft winged curves ending at the corner of the mouth, while the lower is rounded from inside to out and has a central groove separating the lip into two parts from left to right.

## The Ear

The ear is made up of cartilage. There is an outer rim, and an inner elevation in front of which is the hollow of the ear. The opening of the canal is overhung by a flap below which hangs the lobe.

**Illus. 69. Mouth.**

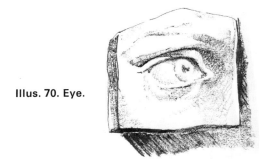

**Illus. 70. Eye.**

**Illus. 68. Ear.**

**Illus. 67. Nose.**

Vertically, the ear is on a line with the back of the jaw. Horizontally, it lies between the brow and the base of the nose.

## The Eye

The eye is not set on the surface. The eye socket is set deeply into the skull and the eyeball fits into the socket. The lower lid is stable and does not move perceptibly, whereas the upper lid does. The upper lid has a bulge because it always partly covers the eyeball.

Eyesockets can be close together or far apart, and lids can be either thick or thin.

As soon as you feel confident that you have

**39**

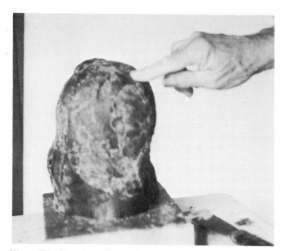

**Illus. 71. Use hands and fingers as well as tools to model.**

into the skin of the skull. Indent and build up where necessary. Work all round and look at your model repeatedly from each angle. Keep firmly fixed in your mind the fact that the skull is underneath and so are the muscles. Always think in terms of basic units and geometric shapes and you will have a feeling of control.

Never depend entirely on your tools. When you want, work with your hands and fingers. As you add and subtract, model and blend, you will see the portrait emerging. This is an exciting moment. Don't be tempted to hurry. Keep a steady pace and don't be careless.

gained an awareness of the inner structure of the head, you are ready to model. Modelling requires an in-and-out movement and a rounding and blending technique. Model all masses into the planes of the face with a wooden tool. Use a small wire tool to dig out places like the corner of the eye, the opening in the ear. Work on the back as well as the front. Make wax pellets, and with your fingers add them where needed.

Dig deeply into the wax to make the eye sockets. Model the eyeballs separately and place them into the sockets. Blend them in carefully.

Treat the hair as a mass. Blend the hair

**Illus. 72. Blend the hair into the skull.**

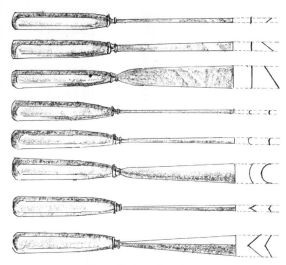

**Illus. 73. Carving tools.**

# Wax Carving

Wax carving is very different from modelling. A carver does not build up—he cuts away. Carving is subtracting and *finding the form within the wax*.

Carving involves cutting down into planes, indenting, curving, rounding off, digging in. Wax carving tools are shown in Illus. 73.

To begin, choose a simple shape such as an elephant that does not require a great deal of detail. Use a solid block of wax (Illus. 74). Wax blocks are 20″ × 10″ × 2″. Depending on the size of your object, you can cut it down or make it thicker by putting two blocks together and running a hot spatula in

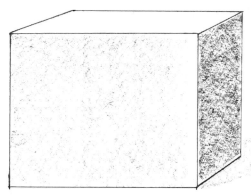

**Illus. 74. Wax block.**

between to make them adhere. Use soft wax for large objects and hard for small ones. It is not necessary to melt wax for carving.

Then, make a charcoal sketch of the elephant. With a penknife or small modelling tool, scratch the profile on both sides of the wax. (You must make sure that the two sides correspond exactly.) Then make another

**Illus. 75. Outline drawing on both sides and back and front.**

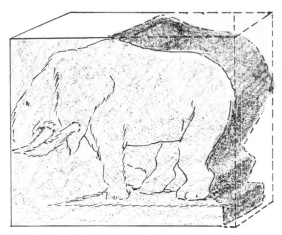

**Illus. 76. Carve away largest masses first.**

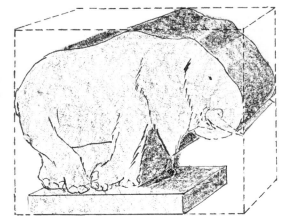

**Illus. 77. Cut and form the most prominent planes.**

sketch of the elephant from the front and one from the back. Scratch these onto the ends of the block.

With large carving tools, both flat and curved, carve and remove the largest masses (Illus. 76), keeping a short distance away from the outline. Now begin to modify the angles, and model and blend with a small modelling tool. Find the most prominent planes first and cut and form contours. Keep blending and softening high, medium, and low planes. Pretend the wax is stone and you cannot add to it—you can only take away.

Attend to details last (Illus. 78). Refine and model each part and relate to other parts by smoothing and blending one plane into another.

Wax carving is excellent training for the more physically demanding stone carving.

**Illus. 78. Leave all the small details until last.**

# Bas Relief

Relief is sometimes called sculptured drawing, or raised drawing. Its depth varies from low, or bas relief, to high, or haut relief. Haut relief can project out from a background to almost full rounded proportions.

To make a bas-relief profile (Illus. 85) in wax, use a block approximately 1 to 2 inches thick, 12 inches wide, and 16 inches high. It is not necessary to melt it. Place the wax

Illus. 79. A bas-relief sculpture.

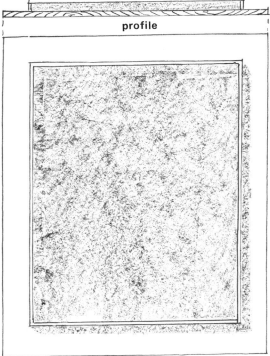

profile

Illus. 80. Use a 2-inch-thick block of wax and place it on a wooden board.

**Illus. 81. Trace your outline onto the wax with a wooden tool.**

**Illus. 82. Scrape round the outline with a wire tool.**

**Illus. 83. Then build up the form by adding bits of wax.**

block on a board, say 14 inches wide and 18 inches high. The board will not only serve as a firm backing while you are working, but can be part of the final frame.

Now, on each side of the wax, nail strips of wood into the board to frame the wax so it will not shift while you are working. Then make a pencil or charcoal sketch of your chosen model in profile. Just as in modelling, note all the important proportions of the head and facial structure and make your measurements with the calipers.

With a wooden tool, copy the outlines of your profile on the wax surface with carbon paper. An important compositional point to

note is that you must place the profile on the wax in such a position that there is more space in front of the face than behind it (Illus. 81). If you don't, it will look as though the profile is "walking" out of the frame. Test this by placing something over the right-hand side of Illus. 81.

Carefully and with a light touch, cut and scrape away the background, beginning round the outline, using a wire modelling tool. Continue until the entire background is cut and smoothed away to an even depth. Do not cut too deeply, for you are going to add wax to the profile.

The next step is to build up the form. Use

bits of wax that are well worked and soft. Add to the high points of the skull first—the cheekbone, the outermost part of the forehead, the temple, the jaw. Press the softened wax on firmly. Add to the middle planes formed by the medium structural points. Fill in all the middle planes, such as between the cheekbone and the jawbone. Add to the ear. Above the eye the forehead is close to you, but recedes above the nose and becomes a lower plane, so add less wax there.

After placing the wax masses, define the planes more accurately. Separate the areas closest to you from those farthest from you. Use a flat wooden tool to do this.

Next, model, that is curve and indent, low points, high points, blend the wax to the contours. Keep the planes distinct, but work one into the other smoothly. Scrape away the background so that it is level all round the relief.

Last, deal with details—the many small planes and curves in the eye, the nose, the mouth, the ear. Every feature must be in proper relationship to the others. The hair is closest to you, then the ear, then the jaw. The outer edge of the eye is closer to you than the inner edge. And, vertically, the inner edge of the eye lines up with the outermost part of the mouth. The tip of the nose and the mid-mouth are the farthest away in profile.

When you have finished and it doesn't look exactly right to you, but you don't know why, check for these common errors:

**Illus. 84 (Left). Fill in the middle planes.**

**Illus. 85 (Right). Add to the points closest to you.**

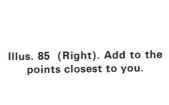

**Illus. 86. An incised bas-relief sculpture. Here, the relief is created by cutting away rather than adding.**

- the inner corner of the eye is too deep;
- the nostril is set too deep;
- the cheekbone is not sufficiently moulded;
- the ear is set too low or too high;
- the underlip and the chin are not separated;
- the hair is not treated as a mass.

**Incised Bas Relief**

Another technique to achieve a bas-relief effect is by incising, that is, cutting away the wax instead of adding to it.

Begin with a sketch as before to use as a guide, and make the wooden base with the strips nailed to it to hold the wax slab. Lightly "draw" your outline on the slab with a wooden modelling tool (Illus. 87).

Start cutting with a wire tool (Illus. 88), beginning along the inside edges of the outline. Cut fairly deep there because it will be the lowest area in the relief. Then establish the most receding points throughout the outline. For the highest points—those closest to you—retain the original wax surface (Illus. 89).

Model the structural planes with a wire tool and refine and blend the modelled planes with a wooden tool. Pay attention to the fine details last. You can make the hair with short and long cutting strokes (Illus. 90).

- the head is too close to the edge of the background;
- the head is curved concavely where it should be convex;

Illus. 87. Draw in the outline.

←

Illus. 88. Cut with wire tool deeply round edge.

→

Illus. 89. Retain original surface for high points.

←

Illus. 90. Make hair with quick strokes of the tool.

→

# INDEX